# CORNISH VILLAGES

*Volume 2*

## Sandra Srivastava

The Book Guild Ltd

First published in Great Britain in 2024 by
The Book Guild Ltd
Unit E2 Airfield Business Park,
Harrison Road, Market Harborough,
Leicestershire. LE16 7UL
Tel: 0116 2792299
www.bookguild.co.uk
Email: info@bookguild.co.uk
X: @bookguild

Copyright © 2024 Sandra Srivastava

The right of Sandra Srivastava to be identified as the author of this
work has been asserted by them in accordance with the
Copyright, Design and Patents Act 1988.

All rights reserved. No part of this publication may be
reproduced, transmitted, or stored in a retrieval system, in any form or by any means,
without permission in writing from the publisher, nor be otherwise circulated in
any form of binding or cover other than that in which it is published and without
a similar condition being imposed on the subsequent purchaser.

Typeset in 11pt Minion Pro

ISBN 978 1835740 002

British Library Cataloguing in Publication Data.
A catalogue record for this book is available from the British Library.

# CORNISH VILLAGES

*Volume 2*

# CONTENTS

*Acknowledgements* ix
*Introduction* xi

Poundstock 1
Crackington Haven 3
Boscastle 7
Port Quin 12
Altarnun 15
Blisland 21
St Agnes 25
Portreath 29
Botallack 33
Sennen Cove 39
Porthcurno 41

| | |
|---|---|
| Mousehole | 45 |
| Flushing | 51 |
| St Clement | 55 |
| Tregony | 57 |
| Portscatho and Gerrans | 61 |
| St Anthony in Roseland | 63 |
| St Mawes | 67 |
| St Just in Roseland | 69 |
| Lerryn | 72 |
| Seaton and Hessenford | 75 |
| Cawsand, Kingsand and Cremyll | 79 |

# ACKNOWLEDGEMENTS

I am most grateful to all members of the team at The Book Guild for their efforts in bringing this project to fruition. In particular, I would like to thank Rosie Lowe, Publishing Manager, and Daniel Burchmore, Production Controller.

# INTRODUCTION

This book is a companion volume to *Cornish Villages*, published in 2023. There are so many fascinating Cornish villages that it would be impossible to mention them all in one volume (or even two). Those included in this book are all over Cornwall so that, wherever you are, there will be somewhere nearby that is well worth visiting. Some of these are in groups, such as those on the Roseland peninsula, since, if you choose one interesting village to visit, you will want to continue to others just down the road, rather than drive past them.

I have also included suggestions for excursions to nearby places so that, if you visit a village that does not occupy a full day, you can combine it with somewhere else.

I have not attempted to recommend eating establishments as they tend to change hands frequently, and because everyone has different tastes and requirements. In recent years, Cornwall has become a 'foodie destination' so, even if your chosen village has few alternatives, you are unlikely to be disappointed.

Happy wanderings!

Sandra Srivastava
October 2023

# POUNDSTOCK

Poundstock is in north Cornwall, 5 mi (8 km) south of Bude. It is a peaceful village with a few scattered houses. It is, however, well worth visiting for St Winwaloe Church and the adjacent Guildhouse (or Gildhouse), both of which are Grade I listed. The church was built in the 13$^{th}$ century on the site of an earlier one; parts were rebuilt in the 15$^{th}$ and 16$^{th}$ centuries, and it was substantially restored in the late 19$^{th}$ century. The north wall of the nave has two large, fascinating, 15$^{th}$-century wall paintings. It is claimed that the church is haunted by the ghost of William Penfound, who was both an assistant curate and a pirate and was murdered in the church by fellow pirates in 1357.

The Guildhouse is a church house with 15$^{th}$-century origins; it was remodelled around the early 16$^{th}$ century, when the attractive mullioned windows were installed. Parish feasts and other social events were held here, and at various times the building has been used as a school, a poorhouse and a meeting place. Remarkably, it has been in continuous use since it was built. It is open to the public on Wednesdays during the summer season but, if you are in the area at other times, even the outside is unmissable.

Beside the Guildhouse is a stone bridge surmounted by a pretty timber lychgate; these are Grade II listed. The bridge is probably 18th-century, and the lychgate is late 19th- or early 20th-century.

## SEE NEARBY

Penhallam Manor is 2.5 mi (4 km) from Poundstock. It is believed to have been built during the 12th–14th centuries. It was abandoned in the 15th century and remained almost forgotten until it was excavated between 1968 and 1973. The outline of the walls was restored and it is now in the care of English Heritage.

# CRACKINGTON HAVEN

Crackington Haven is on the north coast, 7 mi (11 km) north of Boscastle and 10.5 mi (17 km) south of Bude. It is within the Cornwall Area of Outstanding Natural Beauty. It is a small village with a few attractive houses, a pub and cafés, and is popular with walkers and surfers. There is a shingle beach, which has sand and rock pools at low tide. The folded sedimentary rock formations in the cliffs and on the beach make the village a magnet for those interested in geology; the strata are formed from sandstone and grey shales and are known as the 'Crackington formation'.

In the 18th and 19th centuries, limestone and coal were imported here, and slate and other products were exported. Ships were loaded and unloaded on the beach. However, the rough seas made this a hazardous port. When the railways reached Cornwall in the late 19th century, goods could instead be transported to and from larger, safer ports with ease; at the same time, tourism could expand in places like Crackington Haven.

## SEE NEARBY

Marine Drive, a coastal scenic route, takes you from Widemouth Bay to the town of Bude, which has two good beaches and is one of Cornwall's most popular surfing centres.

# BOSCASTLE

Boscastle is a very attractive historic village on the north coast, 14 mi (22.5 km) south of Bude.

There are hotels, shops, cafes, pubs, a National Trust information centre and the Museum of Witchcraft and Magic. This is not nearly as bad as it sounds: the facilities, whilst numerous, are small. The village has been protected from modern development by the steepness of the streets and the valley, the protection of the National Trust, and the fact that it was a Manor Estate until 1946.

The area of the village which is now the busiest is behind the harbour. Parts of the Wellington Hotel are 400 years old. It was a coaching inn until the early 1920s, and was one of the last posting houses in the country. It is now a Grade II listed building. The late-17$^{th}$-century Cobweb Inn is an interesting building on five floors. It was an off-licence, then a warehouse, and was granted a full licence in 1947.

The harbour was built at the head of an S-shaped inlet, which provided shelter from rough seas, but which also made it difficult for larger boats to reach the haven. The inner jetty was built in 1584, when Boscastle was already a prosperous port. The outer jetty was built during the 19th century; it was accidentally destroyed by a stray mine during the Second World War and was rebuilt by the National Trust in 1962.

In 2004 a flash flood caused major damage to the buildings of the harbour area, destroying bridges and sweeping many cars out to sea. Fortunately there were no deaths or serious injuries. In 2007 there was another, less severe, flood. Some preventative works have been carried out, although Boscastle will always be subject to flooding because of its geographical position.

Boscastle takes its name from Bottreaux Castle, built by the Bottreaux family, who came to Cornwall from Normandy at some point after the Norman Conquest of 1066. The castle is believed to date from the 11th and/or 12th centuries and to have been built on high ground overlooking the steep-sided Valency valley. The village developed in the area around the castle, where many 16th- and 17th-century houses remain. The castle itself has now disappeared, but it is possible to visit what is thought to be the castle mound. On the main street, Dunn Street, opposite the community centre is a sign pointing to the 'Site of Bottreaux Castle'. A short path leads to an information board and a small, grassed area with picnic tables. About half of the original castle site has been built over, but stone footings were

discovered here. Richard Carew, in his *Survey of Cornwall* (1602), says that the castle contained a prison with several rooms.

At Penally Point, on the northern side of the harbour entrance, is the Devil's Bellows, a blowhole which, when the sea is rough, shoots water across the harbour entrance about an hour before low tide.

On the promontory of Willapark (not to be confused with its namesake at Tintagel), to the south of the harbour, are the remains of an Iron Age cliff castle, which could easily be defended as it was built on an isthmus, across which a ditch and rampart were constructed.

Nearby are the Forrabury Stitches, a Celtic field pattern now preserved by the National Trust. These are long, narrow fields which are cultivated by tenant farmers in summer and grazed in common during the winter months. This involves a four-year crop rotation system discontinued in other parts in medieval times. The banks between the fields contain many wild flowers that have become rare elsewhere because of modern farming methods. Between the stitches and the village is St Symphorian's church, just south of which is an early Celtic cross.

A footpath leads up the wooded, steep-sided Valency valley towards St Merteriana's (or Merthiana's, or Minster) Church, built on the site of a monastery; there is a holy well and a colony of rare greater horseshoe bats.

## SEE NEARBY

The interesting, but very busy, village of Tintagel is 3.5 mi (5.5 km) down the coast; Tintagel Castle is one of Cornwall's most picturesque. In the opposite direction, Crackington Haven (7 mi, 11 km) has a beautiful beach and is well known for its folded sedimentary rock formations in the cliffs.

# PORT QUIN

Port Quin is a pretty hamlet at the head of a small, exceptionally beautiful inlet on the north coast, between Port Isaac and Polzeath. It is hard to believe that it was once a busy port. It was a fishing village, and slate was exported from here; some residents were employed at local lead and antimony mines. However, all that changed in the late 19th century, when the Cornish pilchard industry declined, the mines failed and the arrival of the railways meant that slate could be transported more easily to larger ports. The village was virtually deserted for decades, and many of the cottages and fish cellars disappeared.

Eventually the National Trust restored some of the remaining buildings and converted them to holiday homes. This included Doyden Castle, a folly built around 1830 on the clifftop as a party venue for local businessman Samuel Symons.

There is a National Trust car park and a small, rocky beach. It is popular with independent kayakers, and it is also possible to book organised kayaking trips to spot wildlife and explore the many small coves.

## SEE NEARBY

Walks along the coast path afford excellent views of Lundy Bay and the countryside. The walk northwards towards Port Isaac is a spectacular but particularly challenging stretch of the coast path. If you do not wish to attempt this walk, it is well worth wandering a short distance up the coast path to enjoy the views of the village and inlet.

Polzeath (3 mi, 5 km) is a popular holiday resort with good surfing.

# ALTARNUN

Altarnun is on the edge of Bodmin Moor, 14.5 mi (23 km) north of Bodmin and 9 mi (14 km) southeast of Launceston. The village and the surrounding area have been occupied since ancient times. It has many very pretty cottages, a village green, two bridges and a famous church.

A packhorse bridge crosses the river; this may have been built in the 15$^{th}$ century or later. It remains very attractive despite having been subject to alteration. In the early 20$^{th}$ century it was widened slightly on the downstream side to accommodate motor vehicles. In the 1970s a new road bridge was built close by, and the old bridge was restored to its original width.

The original church was built in the 6$^{th}$ century, the time of St Nonna, then another was built on the site in the 12$^{th}$ century. Parts of this church remain but most of the present building is 15$^{th}$-century. It is known as the Cathedral of the Moor because of its size. Its tall tower and other parts of the building were constructed

using surface granite from Bodmin Moor. Near the gates is a medieval wheel-headed wayside cross head, which was cemented onto a modern shaft and base around 1905.

On the main street is a type K6 telephone box, a square cast-iron kiosk with a domed roof. This was designed in 1935 and is now a grade II listed building.

A few minutes' walk northwards, in a field, is the famous St Nonna's Well, which was a bowsening pool: attempts were made to cure lunatics by repeatedly pushing them backwards into the water. This took place from the 16$^{th}$ century, if not earlier, and may have continued until the late 19$^{th}$ century, by which time the well was reputedly dry and overgrown.

## SEE NEARBY

At Trewint, 2 mi (3 km) down a lane, is Isbell Cottage, where the preacher John Wesley and his companions stayed on at least six occasions whilst travelling in Cornwall during the 18$^{th}$ century. The Wesley Room is now a small museum.

It is possible to walk to the summit of Brown Willy, the highest point in Cornwall, in the middle of Bodmin Moor; Rough Tor, almost as high, is nearby.

Dozmary Pool, 6 mi (9.5 km) south of Altarnun, is one of the sites associated with the Excalibur legend; King Arthur received the sword, Excalibur, from the Lady of the Lake and it was returned to her by Bedivere when Arthur was on his deathbed. According to another legend, the giant Jan Tregeagle made a pact with the devil and was given money and power; at the end of his life, the mansion and estate were flooded by the pool and he was condemned to bale it out using only a limpet shell with a hole in it.

# BLISLAND

Blisland is a quiet, picturesque village on the western side of Bodmin Moor. A granite church, houses and a pub surround a wooded village green, indicating that this was a Saxon settlement. The village also has a shop, café, doctor's surgery and primary school.

The beautiful, Grade-II*-listed, 16$^{th}$-century Mansion House has two Norman windows and a small Norman arch over a doorway.

The Grade-I-listed Norman church, the only one in Britain to be dedicated to Saints Protus and Hyacinth, is thought to have been built on the site of an earlier Saxon church. The saints were Italian brothers who were martyred in AD260; the remains of St Hyacinth were discovered in the catacombs in 1848 but those of St Protus were no longer there. There is a sundial above the door and it has an ornate, whitewashed interior with a wagon roof.

On the eastern edge of the village, beside the road, are St Pratt's cross and holy well (St Pratt is the local name for St Protus); there is a feast day procession from the church to these on 22nd September each year.

South of the village are footpaths through the ancient Lavethan Wood, a nature reserve managed by the Woodland Trust. It is designated a Planted Ancient Woodland Site and an Area of Outstanding Natural Beauty. It is full of bluebells in spring.

North of the village is the Grade-II-listed Jubilee Rock, a volcanic rock about 10 ft (3 m) high and 25 ft (7.6 m) across. In 1810 Lieutenant John Rogers of the 65th Regiment designed the carvings of coats of arms and insignia on the rock to celebrate the golden jubilee of George III. In 2010 Blisland Parish Council celebrated the 200th anniversary of the carvings by restoring them and refixing the original brass plate.

## SEE NEARBY

The start of the Camel Trail is 2 mi (3 km) away, at Wenford Bridge. This is an 18-mi (29-km) trail for walkers, wheelchair users, cyclists and horse riders along a former railway line to Padstow.

Bodmin Jail is 6 mi (9.5 km). This was a notorious prison from 1779 to 1922, during which time 55 hangings took place here. It has now become a visitor attraction and a 70-room hotel. It is reputed to be Britain's most-haunted building; you can even get married here, if you dare.

# ST AGNES

St Agnes is a large village on the north coast, 4 mi (6.5 km) southwest of Perranporth. The surrounding area is nationally important for its fauna and flora including seals, seabirds, coral, butterflies and rare plants; it is a Special Area of Conservation, a Site of Special Scientific Interest and a voluntary Marine Conservation Area, and is within the Cornwall Area of Outstanding Natural Beauty.

St Agnes is part of the Cornwall and West Devon Mining Landscape World Heritage Site and is on the St Agnes Heritage Coast. There was mining in the area from the Bronze Age until the early 20th century. It was well known for the quality of its tin, and was also important for copper and arsenic. Many of the properties on the steep streets of St Agnes are former miners' cottages and mine owners' houses. In the centre of the village is St Agnes Museum, with displays relating to mining, farming and the natural history of the area. There is a good range of local services including excellent hotels, restaurants and shops.

The remains of mine workings can be seen along the road down the valley leading northwards from the village centre to Trevaunance Cove. Overlooking the valley are the remains of engine houses. Trevaunance Cove has interesting old cottages and several popular eating establishments. Over the centuries, five harbours were built here for the export of tin and copper ore, the import of coal and timber, and to support the pilchard fishing industry. Each successive harbour was eventually swept away by the sea, the last one during the storms of 1915–16. Since it was no longer needed, it was not rebuilt. Granite blocks and foundations, the remains of these harbours, can be seen on the western side of the beach at low tide. The cove has instead become popular with surfers and bathers.

From the village, Beacon Drive takes you towards Chapel Porth and St Agnes Beacon. On a right hand bend, go straight ahead to Chapel Porth, where there is a National Trust car park, a small café, toilets and a popular bathing and surfing beach. From here, the south west coast path leads northwards towards Trevaunance Cove, past the foundations of an 11$^{th}$-century chapel and the famous Towanroath engine house, where water was pumped from nearby Wheal Coates mine. A path leads upwards to the fascinating remains of Wheal Coates on the clifftop. Alternatively, after visiting Chapel Porth, return to Beacon Drive and turn left. On the left side of the road is a National Trust car park close to Wheal Coates.

On the opposite side of Beacon Drive from the car park is a path leading to the summit of St Agnes Beacon, a distance of about 0.4 mi (0.6 km), through heather

and gorse. From the summit are far-reaching views over the north coast and St Agnes; a number of engine houses and chimneys are still standing in and around the village. On a clear day there are also views of Carn Brea, the south coast and much of Cornwall. At night, 12 lighthouses can be seen.

## SEE NEARBY

St Piran's Round, or Perran Round, is 5.5 mi (9 km) from St Agnes. It is believed to be a late prehistoric enclosure for an agricultural settlement, repurposed in the Middle Ages for performances of Cornish miracle plays. It is a scheduled monument.

Tehidy Country Park (9 mi, 15 km) has woodland walks, lakes, abundant wildlife and spectacular displays of bluebells in late April and early May.

There are excellent surfing beaches at the popular holiday resorts of Porthtowan (4 mi, 6.5 km), Perranporth (4 mi, 6.5 km) and Newquay (11.5 mi, 18.5 km).

# PORTREATH

Portreath is on the north coast, 4.5 mi (7 km) from Redruth. It is a popular surfing centre with a large sandy beach, small harbour and coastal walks. There are numerous shops and eating establishments.

Portreath had been a small fishing village for centuries until, in 1713, a harbour was built at the western side of the beach. This was destroyed by rough seas and, in 1760, the present harbour was built at the eastern side of the beach to serve the copper mining industry, so that ships no longer had to be loaded and unloaded on the beach. In the early 19th century, improvements were made to the harbour and mineral tramways were built, linking Portreath with the mines of St Day and Scorrier. Portreath port became one of the most important in Cornwall. Copper ore was exported to Swansea, and coal and timber were brought back for use in the mines.

The entrance to this narrow harbour was dangerous for shipping. The Pepperpot, a white conical tower on the clifftop, was built in the 19th century

as a daymark to guide ships into the harbour, and at night a small light was shown on the hill.

The small stone whitewashed building at the end of the pier is known locally as the Monkey Hut or Monkey House. The original building was constructed in the 19th century as a shelter for the harbour pilot, who would guide ships into the harbour or warn them away if the sea was too rough. It was washed away by high seas in 2014 and was replaced the same year. The harbour wall suffered severe damage in the same storm, and the pier is now fenced off.

The Cornish mining industry declined from the mid-19th century, when copper and tin could be mined more economically in other parts of the world. The harbour was still used for the import of coal, slate, cement and potatoes until the mid-20th century, but is now used seasonally by fishing and leisure boats; in winter, many of the boats are craned out of the water.

At low tide, rock pools can be explored at the harbour end of the beach and caves at the other end.

Just offshore is Gull Rock, so named because it is frequented by numerous gulls.

Every few years a petrified forest becomes visible on the beach when there is a storm at the same time as an exceptionally low tide. This forest is believed to date back to Neolithic times, about 4000 to 6000 years ago, and was submerged when sea levels rose. The remains of the trees were compressed by mud, peat or sand and became petrified. Today, only stumps and roots remain.

## SEE NEARBY

Walkers, horseriders and cyclists can enjoy the Coast to Coast Trail, which connects Portreath with Devoran, on the south coast, and the Portreath Branchline Trail between Portreath and Brea, near Redruth.

Tehidy Country Park and golf course are close by.

Godrevy Point is 6.5 mi (10.5 km) south-west of Portreath on the coast path, and a similar distance by road. A large colony of grey seals can be seen here throughout the year, up to 100 in January. Godrevy Island is just offshore; its lighthouse is believed to have been the inspiration for Virginia Woolf's novel, *To The Lighthouse*.

# BOTALLACK

Botallack is 8 mi (12.5 km) west of Penzance on the B3306, a spectacular stretch of road close to the north coast between St Ives and Sennen. It is a quiet former mining village with many attractive granite cottages. The early 18$^{th}$-century Queen's Arms in the centre of the village is a Grade II listed building.

Botallack Manor House, on the northern edge of the village, is a beautiful, small, Grade II* listed building constructed in 1665. The rear of the house was used in the filming of the 1970s TV series, *Poldark*. The front was not used because electricity cables were visible, so nearby Pendeen Manor was used instead.

There was mining along the coast here between the 16$^{th}$ and 20$^{th}$ centuries and is believed to have been carried on in the Roman period, around 200 AD, when the Romans came to Cornwall in search of tin. There may even have been mining here in the Bronze Age. Tin, copper and arsenic were produced at Botallack Mine. In the mining heyday of the 19$^{th}$ century, tunnels extended beneath the seabed

for up to half a mile; the mine had 11 engine houses and employed 500 people. Work continued day and night and there was much noise, smoke and dirty water. However, Cornish mining declined in the late 19$^{th}$ century, when low tin and copper prices meant that the mines were running at a loss. Mines closed and many skilled miners emigrated to countries such as Australia, North America, Mexico and South Africa, where mining costs were lower and their skills were in demand. Botallack Mine closed in 1895, re-opened in the early 20$^{th}$ century and closed finally in 1914.

Today, there is much to see at Botallack Mine. The site is now owned by the National Trust and is part of the Cornwall and West Devon Mining Landscape, which is a UNESCO World Heritage Site. Clinging to the cliffside are two iconic and much-photographed engine houses, the Crowns engine houses; only the upper one is accessible to visitors. These and the Count House are Grade II listed buildings. The Count House, built in the mid-19$^{th}$ century, was the mine office. It was built in a grand style in order to instil confidence in potential investors. It now houses mining displays and a small café. Nearby are chimney stacks and an arsenic labyrinth. Looking southwards, you can see West Wheal Owles and Wheal Edwards engine houses, and just inland from these is Wheal Owles, where 20 people lost their lives in a mining accident in 1893.

If you come here in August or September, bring a container, because the blackberries are the best in Cornwall.

## SEE NEARBY

The town of St Just-in-Penwith is 1 mi (1.5 km) south of Botallack. This has numerous shops and eateries and a pretty church. In the centre of the town is the Plain-an-Gwarry, or 'playing place', which is a scheduled monument. This may have been constructed during the Iron Age as an enclosed farming settlement; in medieval times it was used as an open-air theatre, and public events are now held here.

From St Just it is a further 1.5 mi (2.5 km) to Cape Cornwall, which has a few attractive houses, a large National Trust car park, a café and toilets. In an enclosure is the ruined medieval St Helen's Oratory, believed to have been built on the site of a 6th-century church; this is now a scheduled monument. On the headland is a steep path up to a coastguard lookout, and on the summit is a chimney stack which was built in 1850 for Cape Cornwall Mine.

If you are interested in Cornwall's mining history, Levant (National Trust) and Geevor mines, just north of Botallack, are well worth visiting.

# SENNEN COVE

Sennen Cove is 2 mi (3 km) from Land's End and 9 mi (14.5 km) from Penzance, and is the westernmost village in mainland England. It is still a fishing village, although little fishing takes place in winter because of the severity of the weather on this exposed coast. There are pretty cottages, a jetty and a lifeboat station.

The famous Round House is a Grade II* listed building. It was built from stone and wood to house the capstan, probably in the 18th century, and the capstan remains in remarkable condition. An upper floor was added in the 19th century as a fishermen's store. Both floors are now used as a gallery and shop.

There is a large sandy beach and, at low tide, you can walk northwards from here to Gwenver Beach, popular with serious surfers.

## SEE NEARBY

It is possible to walk southwards along the coast path to Land's End, or northwards to Cape Cornwall. South of Sennen Cove is Maen Castle, one of the oldest Iron Age cliff castles in Cornwall; a 12-ft (3.7-metre)-thick wall across the neck of the promontory has post holes at the entrance, indicating that there were once timber gates.

# PORTHCURNO

Porthcurno is 9 mi (14.5 km) south-west of Penzance. It has a few houses, a hotel and a café along a steep-sided valley running down to the sea. There is a large, sandy beach with cliffs on both sides and a stream running along the western side to the sea.

Overlooking the valley, close to the car park, is a large, white building which is the multi-award-winning Museum of Global Communications, opened in 1998. The first international telegraph cable was landed at Porthcurno in 1870, and messages now took nine minutes instead of six weeks to reach India. In 1872 the Eastern Telegraph Company was formed. More cables followed, and Porthcurno Telegraph Station became the world's most important station. During World War II it was realised that the station was very vulnerable to enemy attack; tunnels were dug into the hillside and operations were moved underground. With technological advancements, the station ceased operating in 1970, although a training college remained on the site until 1993.

On the western clifftop is the Minack Theatre, a Grecian-style amphitheatre hewn out of the cliff in the 1930s by Rowena Cade, with her bare hands and those of her gardener. Open air performances take place here in all weathers during summer evenings; actors have been known to perform in their raincoats to preserve their costumes for future performances. Many audience members take cushions, blankets, strawberries and cream and wine and enjoy trying to spot whales and dolphins before the start of the performance (it is dark by the time of the interval). Throughout the year it is possible to visit the theatre during the day in order to appreciate its spectacular setting.

On the eastern side of the bay is the headland of Treryn Dinas, accessed along the coast path. This is the 36-ac (14.5 ha) site of an Iron Age cliff castle, where a number of defensive ditches and ramparts and a causewayed entrance can still be seen.

On the tip of the headland is the Logan Rock (one of several in Cornwall), which is an 80-ton (73-tonne) boulder that can be rocked with great difficulty. According to legend, people accused of crimes were once tried here, since it was said that no criminal could move the rock. It was much easier to rock until, in 1824, a young naval officer pushed it down the cliff as a prank. The Admiralty made him replace it at his own expense but provided equipment for him to do so. However, he was unable to position it so that it rocked as easily as it had done.

## SEE NEARBY

Penberth Cove is an exceptionally pretty hamlet, 2.5 mi (4 km) by road or 1.5 mi (2.5 km) along the coast path. There are a few cottages, fishing boats lined up on the shore, and a restored 19th-century capstan which was used to drag boats out of the sea.

The Merry Maidens stone circle is 5 mi (8 km) from Porthcurno. Each of the 19 stones is approximately 4 ft (1.2 m) high. Legend has it that these were maidens who were turned to stone for dancing on a Sunday. About 1000 ft (300 m) away are two standing stones, each 10 ft (3 m) high, known as the Pipers, who were said to have played for the dancers. Further legends attempt to explain the distance between the two sites; either the musicians were running away from the maidens because they realised it was just after midnight and they would be breaking the Sabbath, or the two stones were erected separately to commemorate Howel and Athelstan, who died in battle in the 10th century.

# MOUSEHOLE

Mousehole (pronounced 'Mowzle') is a former fishing village, 3.5 mi (5.5 km) from Penzance. Cornwall's first pier was built here in approximately AD 400. It was an important port until the decline of the fishing industry in the early 20th century.

The centre of the village is a warren of little granite cottages in narrow streets overlooking a pretty harbour, with a sandy beach at low tide. Not surprisingly, it was one of the villages of west Cornwall which became popular with artists, who visited or moved here from the late 19th century onwards to paint the 'picturesque' villages and the everyday lives of the fisherfolk. Consequently it has become highly popular with tourists, who are now the major source of income for the villagers. Nowadays there is little commercial fishing. The little boats in the harbour are pleasure craft, and it is possible to go on fishing or sightseeing trips.

On Keigwin Place is a very attractive 16th-century manor house. Part of the upper storey is supported on four granite pillars and a massive, moulded

granite doorway also survives. When Spanish marauders burned Mousehole to the ground in 1595, this was the only building left standing. Its owner, Jenkin Keigwin, was reputedly struck by a cannonball fired from one of the Spanish ships before the marauders landed. It later became the Keigwin Arms and is now a private residence. Although almost all of the residents of Mousehole lost their homes, very few were killed. The attack was intended not as another invasion, but as revenge for the defeat of the Spanish Armada. Newlyn, Paul and part of Penzance were also destroyed.

Also on Keigwin Place, overlooking the harbour, is the home of Dolly Pentreath. A plaque on the wall reads: 'Here lived Dolly Pentreath one of the last speakers of the Cornish language as her native tongue died Dec. 1777.' Mousehole, being in the far west of Cornwall, was naturally one of the last places where the Cornish language was spoken on a day-to-day basis. Local legend has it that Dolly was the last person to speak only Cornish (she claimed to have spoken no English until the age of 20), although others continued to speak both Cornish and English for another century or so. There is a memorial to Dolly set into the wall of Paul churchyard, where she is buried.

In winter the harbour entrance is closed off by massive timber baulks in order to protect the harbour from storms. From mid-December, boats in the harbour, as well as the streets of the village, are decorated with the world-famous Mousehole lights, which visitors travel long distances to see. On 19th December each year,

most of the Christmas lights are turned off for an hour in memory of the eight-man crew of the Penlee lifeboat, the *Solomon Browne,* who were lost on that day in 1981, whilst trying to rescue the crew of the *Union Star*. The money for a new lifeboat was raised within days; the *Mabel Alice* is moored in Newlyn harbour, and the old lifeboat house in Mousehole has been preserved.

On 23$^{rd}$ December Tom Bawcock's Eve is celebrated. Although there is no proof that Tom really existed or that the story is true, he is supposed to have bravely gone out fishing on 23$^{rd}$ December some time in the 16$^{th}$ century, when long-lasting high storms had prevented fishermen from going out and the villagers were close to starvation. He returned with enough fish to feed the whole village. Each year the villagers eat 'star-gazy pie', a pie made with whole fish with their heads sticking straight up out of the pastry, as if gazing at the stars. However, there was such a custom before the supposed time of Tom Bawcock; a pie was baked using different types of fish, representing the hopes of the fishermen for the year to come.

St Clement's Isle, a small island off Mousehole, is named after St Clement, a hermit who lived on the island and is said to have maintained a light to warn shipping. Just offshore at the southern end of the village is Merlyn Rock. Legend has it that King Arthur dined here after being summoned into battle, although there is a rock with a similar legend near Sennen. Nearby is the cave known as the Mousehole. The harbour entrance has also been called a 'mousehole' because it is so difficult for boats to squeeze through the gap between the quays.

## SEE NEARBY

Newlyn is a busy fishing town; the harbour is spectacular on a sunny day. From here it is a short, pleasant walk along the seafront to Penzance, an interesting town with numerous shops and eating establishments.

# FLUSHING

Flushing is 3 mi (5 km) east of Penryn; this is not to be confused with a smaller Flushing, 3 mi (5 km) east of Helford. The best way to arrive here is by ferry from Falmouth; the views of Flushing and Falmouth from the water are unmissable. Alternatively, there is easy roadside parking before you reach the very narrow streets.

The village began in 1661 when the Trefusis family, local landowners, decided to develop a harbour and brought over Dutch engineers, who named the village after their home town, Vlissingen, known in English as Flushing. They used their expertise in land reclamation to construct three piers and part of the village on faggots after draining several acres of swampy ground. In the 17$^{th}$ to 19$^{th}$ centuries, Flushing and Falmouth were the centre of an international mail service; this ended when the railways reached larger towns and cities on the south coast of England. Many of the captains of the packet ships made their fortunes and their homes here; a number of naval officers also built houses here.

Thanks to its elegant houses and its very mild climate, the village remains a desirable place to live. It is a sailing paradise and holds an annual regatta.

Along the narrow streets in the centre of the village are many attractive cottages, pubs and shops.

At Trefusis Point, on the southern edge of the village, is a sandy beach with spectacular views across the mouth of the Penryn River towards Falmouth.

## SEE NEARBY

Falmouth is an excellent place to visit if you love food. It also has safe beaches, the English Heritage-run Pendennis Castle and the world-famous National Maritime Museum Cornwall.

# ST CLEMENT

St Clement is 2 mi (3 km) east of Truro. It is on the Tresillian River, a peaceful tidal creek with woodland on either side. There has been a settlement here at least as far back as the Domesday Book of 1086; in times gone by, the inhabitants were farmers and fishermen. It has a number of very pretty cottages, some overlooking the creek.

The church is a Grade I listed building, built in the 15th century and restored in the 19th. The famous Ignioc Stone granite monument stands in the churchyard, close to the south wall of the church. The monolith itself is from the Roman period, possibly 3rd century, but the three inscriptions are thought to date from the 6th to 13th centuries. It is now a Grade II* listed building and a scheduled monument.

The two-storey lychgate is 18th-century with 19th-century alterations, and is a Grade II listed building, as are the cottages on both sides of it and a number of other cottages in the village.

## SEE NEARBY

There is an easy walk from St Clement along a level, creekside footpath to Tresillian, a distance of about 2 mi (3 km). Herons, curlews and other waterbirds are easy to spot on and around the creek.

Truro is Cornwall's only city. It has a cathedral, a museum and Cornwall's best shops, all within a small area that is easy to explore on foot.

# TREGONY

Tregony is an elegant village, 8 mi (12.5 km) from Truro and 8.5 mi (14 km) from St Austell. It has a broad main street (Tregony Hill and Fore Street) with pretty colour-washed houses, two churches, a clock tower, almshouses, a pub, a shop and an art gallery.

There was a Norman castle on what is now Tregony Hill but nothing remains of it, not even a mound. A priory and a chapel have also disappeared. Tregony was once an important port and had a market and a wool factory. However, it declined after the 17th century, when tin mining and china clay works upstream caused the River Fal to become so silted up that barges could not reach the town. It proved impossible to deepen the channel, and the town eventually became the quiet village that you see today.

The striking almshouses known as The Gallery, on Tregony Hill, were constructed in 1696 and rebuilt in 1895, when the wooden balcony was added, supported on granite pillars. A row of privies can still be seen at the bottom of the communal back garden. The building now comprises six flatlets for elderly people and is Grade II*-listed.

Adjacent to the almshouses is the Grade-II-listed Castle Cottage, probably built in the 17$^{th}$ century. This was formerly a prison.

One of the most attractive buildings in the village is the iconic 17$^{th}$-century clock tower on Fore Street. This was rebuilt in the 19$^{th}$ century and is now a Grade II listed building.

## SEE NEARBY

Tregony is close to the south coast fishing villages of St Mawes, Portscatho, Portloe, Gorran Haven and Mevagissey.

# PORTSCATHO AND GERRANS

Portscatho is on the Roseland peninsula, 5.5 mi (9 km) from St Mawes. The peninsula is within the Cornwall Area of Outstanding Natural Beauty.

Portscatho is a typical attractive fishing village with tiny whitewashed cottages close to the harbour. There is now very little fishing, but it has become a popular tourist destination and there are shops, galleries, restaurants and a pub. On The Lugger are terraces of elegant houses. Opposite these, overlooking the harbour, is a small square building that was formerly a fishermen's shelter and now hosts art exhibitions. There is a small beach with rock pools; north of the village, accessed along the coast path, is a larger sandy beach with a café and toilets.

Adjoining Porthscatho on the landward side is the village of Gerrans, with traditional Cornish cottages, a pub and a small heritage centre. The pretty church was built in the 13$^{th}$ century and the spire added in the 15$^{th}$ as a daymark for shipping.

## SEE NEARBY

Towan Beach is 2 mi (3 km) south of Portscatho. This is a sand and shingle beach, with rock pools at low tide.

Trelissick, a large National Trust property, is 5 mi (8 km) north of Portscatho. Visitors can enjoy the gardens, woodland walks and sometimes the ground floor of the house.

# ST ANTHONY IN ROSELAND

St Anthony in Roseland is a small, scattered settlement on the Roseland peninsula, 17.5 mi (28 km) from Truro. It includes St Anthony Head, the Place Estate and several farms.

St Anthony Head is owned by the National Trust. The coastal artillery fort was built in the late 19th and early 20th centuries to defend the Fal estuary from invasion. The officers' quarters are now holiday homes. From the nearby bird hide it is possible to observe seals, cormorants, shags and many other seabirds. Perched on the tip of the headland is the 19th-century St Anthony Lighthouse; this is no longer open to the public as it is now a holiday home.

The Grade-II-listed Place House, formerly called Place Manor, is a beautiful, romantic building. It has 13th-century origins and was mostly remodelled and extended in a French gothic style in the 19th century. The house became a hotel after World War II; together with several cottages on the estate, it is now a holiday home.

The adjoining Grade II*-listed Church of St Anthony was similarly built in the 13th century and extensively restored in the 19th.

There is a seasonal ferry between Place Creek and St Mawes; this takes about 10 minutes and is a spectacular ride in sunny weather, with views of blue seas and white sails.

A particularly attractive section of the South West Coast Path follows the coast around the peninsula. Close to St Anthony Head, accessible from the coast path, are Little and Great Molunan beaches.

## SEE NEARBY

At the northern end of the Roseland are Pendower and Carne beaches (5.5 mi, 9 km).

Veryan (7 mi, 11.5 km) is a very attractive village with a pub, a shop, a village green, a park and, of course, the famous round houses, built in the 19th century with no corners for the devil to hide behind.

# ST MAWES

St Mawes is on the Roseland peninsula, 18.5 mi (30 km) from Truro. Although St Mawes was once an important town, it is now officially a village, but is occasionally referred to as a town because it is so large. At the 2021 census, the full-time population was only 644, and the majority of the houses are holiday homes. It is an upmarket village and a yachting paradise, with a variety of hotels, restaurants and shops. Overlooking the harbour, and on narrow streets off the seafront road, are some very attractive 17th- and 18th-century cottages, some thatched.

The castle is a Grade I listed building and a scheduled monument, and is under the care of English Heritage. It was constructed in 1542 by Henry VIII, who built a number of castles along the south coast for defence against attack by the French and Spanish. Together with a larger castle at Falmouth, it defended the entrance to the River Fal. It has a central round tower and three semi-circular bastions; this shape gave it a wide field of fire and enabled it to deflect cannonballs. It had a garrison of up to a hundred men in times of war; this brought much trade to the village, and the population increased enormously. In the 18th and 19th centuries the pilchard and boatbuilding industries thrived here, and there was much smuggling of tobacco, spirits, clothes and fine fabrics.

On Commercial Road, opposite the top of Bohella Road, is a holy well dedicated to Saint Mawes or Mauditus. The well itself may date back to the 6th century, although the well house has a medieval stone arch and a 20th-century carved and inscribed oak door. It is a Grade II listed building and a scheduled monument. The 19th-century house to the left of the well is Holy Well Cottage, which was possibly built on the foundations of a medieval chapel.

## SEE NEARBY

There is a foot ferry between St Mawes and Falmouth, a very pleasant town with a mild climate, good beaches and plentiful restaurants.

There is a particularly pretty coastal walk from St Mawes Castle to the village of St Just in Roseland, a distance of about 2.5 mi (4 km).

# ST JUST IN ROSELAND

St Just in Roseland is on the Roseland peninsula, 2.5 mi (4 km) north of St Mawes. The centre of the village has some attractive old cottages, but the main places of interest are the church and the creek area.

The church is away from the centre of population, down a lane. It was established around AD 550 by Saint Just. The present building was consecrated in 1261, there was much rebuilding in the early 15th century, and it was restored in 1872. It is a Grade I listed building. The 18th-century rectory is Grade II* listed. The two lychgates are 17th-century, possibly rebuilt in the early 19th century; both are Grade II listed. The holy well is a Grade II listed building and a scheduled monument.

The churchyard is well known for its interesting variety of plants, including hydrangeas, fuchsias and many subtropical plants. It slopes steeply down to the shore of St Just Creek, where in times gone by there was a small fishing fleet and, in the 19th century, quarantine ships were anchored. Nowadays the boatyard caters for the many small pleasure craft.

## SEE NEARBY

St Anthony Head (7 mi, 11.5 km) has a battery and a lighthouse; cormorants, shags and seals can be spotted here.

Portscatho (3 mi, 5 km) is a pleasant village with a popular beach.

# LERRYN

Lerryn is approximately 3 mi (5 km) from Lostwithiel. It is an attractive village with many interesting old buildings on both sides of the River Lerryn, a creek of the River Fowey. There is an 18$^{th}$-century pub, a shop, toilets and a car park. Beware, though – the car park sometimes floods during very high tides.

Lerryn was once a busy port. There has been a bridge here at least as far back as 1289, but it was rebuilt in 1575, financed by taxes levied by Queen Elizabeth I in order to aid the silver smelting industry. The river became silted and Lerryn has had no commercial river traffic since 1939. The bridge is now a Grade II* listed building and a scheduled monument. Nearby are stepping stones where the river can be crossed at low tide.

Smuggling was rife here in the 18$^{th}$ and early 19$^{th}$ centuries, due to its out-of-the-way location. However, after the end of the war with France, the Government was free to clamp down on smuggling and it became far less prevalent.

The area around the creek is within the Cornwall Area of Outstanding Natural Beauty and is frequented by ducks, swans, gulls, herons and kingfishers. The river banks are steep and wooded, with popular footpaths. The area north of the river is thought to have been the inspiration for Kenneth Grahame's classic children's novel *The Wind in the Willows* (1908). A popular walk follows a footpath through Ethy Wood, around St Winnow Point, to the village of St Winnow, past St Winnow Mill and back to Lerryn. South of the river, the woodland path passes ruined fountains, arches and swimming pool which are the remains of a pleasure park, Tivoli Park, inspired by the world-famous Tivoli Gardens in Copenhagen and opened in 1922.

## SEE NEARBY

The small, very attractive town of Lostwithiel is well known for its antique shops. The beautiful medieval Lostwithiel Bridge, on North Street, is a Grade I listed building and a scheduled monument. The original bridge was built in the 12th century by the Normans, but it has been rebuilt and repaired several times. The ruins of Restormel Castle are just outside the town.

# SEATON AND HESSENFORD

Seaton is on the south-eastern coast, 5 mi (8 km) from Looe and 9 mi (14.5 km) from Liskeard. Hessenford is 2.5 mi (4 km) north of Seaton.

Despite its small size, Seaton has several eating establishments, toilets, good parking and lifeguards. On arrival, the most striking aspect is its expanse of grey sand and shingle. So long as you do not mind its appearance, this beach is ideal for families.

Seaton Valley Countryside Park, at the bottom of the valley between Seaton and Hessenford, is owned by Cornwall Council. It includes two local nature reserves and has ponds, a sensory garden, woodland and grassland. It is a haven for wildlife including otters, kingfishers and butterflies.

It is well worth walking up the wooded valley to Hessenford; this takes approximately an hour each way. Hessenford has 17th- and 18th-century cottages and a pretty 19th-century church. The popular pub was an early-17th-century coaching inn. The much-photographed three-arched bridge over the River Seaton is late-18th-century and is a Grade II listed building.

If you visit in early May, do not miss the spectacular bluebells. On your way back to Seaton, take the path which diverts to the left from the main footpath. This initially leads uphill and back towards Hessenford, then loops towards Seaton and rejoins the main path, adding about half a mile to your walk.

## SEE NEARBY

At low tide it is possible to walk eastwards along the beach to Downderry. It is also possible to walk along the road or the top of the sea wall, but both are dangerous!

The Monkey Sanctuary is 2 mi (3 km) to the west. This is a rescue centre which cares for about 40 monkeys including woolly monkeys, macaques, capuchins and marmosets.

The town of Looe is 5 mi (8 km) westwards. This is very popular all year but has good parking and plenty of shops and eateries.

# CAWSAND, KINGSAND AND CREMYLL

The villages of Cawsand, Kingsand and Cremyll are described together in this book because you are likely to explore them in one visit rather than separately.

The adjoining picturesque former fishing villages of Cawsand and Kingsand, with painted houses and narrow streets, are on the Rame Peninsula in southeast Cornwall. From Saxon times until 1844, Cawsand was in Cornwall and Kingsand in Devon. The Saxons wished to control both sides of the River Tamar in case of attack by Viking raiders and, in later times, Plymouth Sound remained strategically important. The boundary between Cornwall and Devon was along a small stream between the villages, and one can still see a boundary marker on a cottage on Garrett Street, opposite the Halfway House Inn. It was not until 1844 that the boundary was placed at the Tamar, two miles to the north of the villages, so that both are now in Cornwall.

Because of its proximity to Plymouth, this part of Cornwall was the most notorious for smuggling, which was at its peak in the late 18th and early 19th centuries. Brandy, silk and tobacco were imported and transported to Plymouth for sale. However, after the end of the war with France, the Crown established a preventative service, which was largely successful in clamping down on smuggling. The known smuggling tunnels have been filled in, but some may remain beneath the streets and houses.

The historic part of Cawsand and Kingsand is within a conservation area, and the villages have 85 Grade II listed buildings and structures. One of these is the Maker and Rame Institute and Clock Tower, on the seafront at Kingsand. The clock tower was erected in 1911, attached to an existing building, to commemorate the coronation of King George V. Along with many surrounding houses, it was severely damaged by storms in 2014. It has been repaired and the sea wall strengthened.

On high ground overlooking the bay is the huge, grey Cawsand Fort, a 19th-century fort and battery. It is a Grade II listed building and a scheduled monument. It has now been converted into apartments.

The villages have three sand and shingle beaches, and there are rockpools to explore.

Since the villages are surrounded by Mount Edgcumbe Country Park, there has been little development of the area. The Park is listed as Grade I on the National Register of Historic Parks and Gardens. You can walk northwards from Kingsand on the South West Coast Path through the 885-acre (358-hectare) country park, which contains deer, follies, fountains and other interesting structures, towards the village of Cremyll, in a beautiful setting overlooking Plymouth Sound. This is a small, attractive village with old houses, a pub and a passenger ferry to Plymouth. On the edge of the village is the 16th-century Mount Edgcumbe House and its 18th-century formal gardens. The house was severely damaged by an incendiary bomb during World War II, and was restored between 1958 and 1964. Since 1971 the estate has been owned jointly by Cornwall Council and Plymouth City Council. The park and formal gardens are open all year free of charge, and the house and Earl's Garden are open during the summer months (charge applies).

## SEE NEARBY

It is possible to walk southwards from Cawsand along Earl's Drive through woods to Penlee Point. On the clifftop here is the Old Signal House, built in the late 19th century to house lighthouse keepers. Above this is Penlee Battery, also constructed in the late 19th century. Much of this has been demolished and is now a 17-ac (7-ha) nature reserve comprising woodland and coastal grassland. It is a further half an hour's walk to Rame Head, where there are the remains of an Iron Age cliff castle. On the summit is the 14th-century St Michael's chapel.

Do not miss the scenic drive westwards along Military Road, with Whitsand Bay on your left, overlooked by the massive, 19th-century Tregantle Fort on your right. The fort is still in use by the Ministry of Defence, so you cannot enter, but the outside is well worth exploring.

BV - #0072 - 300524 - C94 - 160/160/7 - PB - 9781835740002 - Gloss Lamination